We Need Custodians

by Jane Scoggins Bauld

Consulting Editor: Gail Saunders-Smith, Ph.D.

Consultant: J. Kirk Campbell, Director of Maintenance
and Custodial Services, Carleton College
Faculty Member, Institute for Facilities Management,
Association of Higher Education Facilities Officers

Pebble Books

an imprint of Capstone Press
Mankato, Minnesota

Pebble Books are published by Capstone Press
151 Good Counsel Drive, P.O. Box 669, Mankato, Minnesota 56002
http://www.capstone-press.com

1 2 3 4 5 6 05 04 03 02 01 00

Library of Congress Cataloging-in-Publication Data
Bauld, Jane Scoggins.
    We need custodians/by Jane Scoggins Bauld.
    p. cm.—(Helpers in our school)
    Includes bibliographical references and index.
    Summary: Simple text and photographs present custodians and their role in
elementary schools.
    ISBN 0-7368-0530-3
    1. School custodians—Juvenile literature. [1. School custodians.] I. Title.
II. Series.
LB3235.B38   2000
372.16′8—dc21   99-047365

Note to Parents and Teachers

The series Helpers in Our School supports national social studies
standards for how groups and institutions work to meet individual
needs. This book describes custodians and illustrates what they do
in schools. The photographs support early readers in understanding
the text. The repetition of words and phrases helps early readers
learn new words. This book also introduces early readers to subject-
specific vocabulary words, which are defined in the Words to Know
section. Early readers may need assistance to read some words and
to use the Table of Contents, Words to Know, Read More, Internet
Sites, and Index/Word List sections of the book.

Table of Contents

Custodians take care
of schools.

Custodians sweep floors.

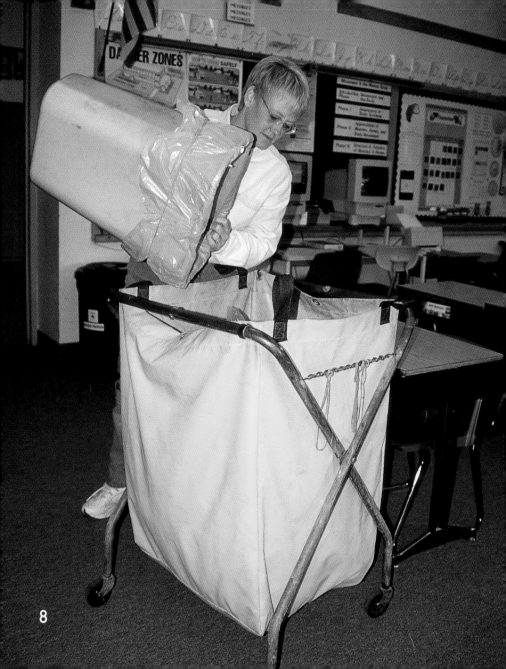

8

Custodians gather trash.

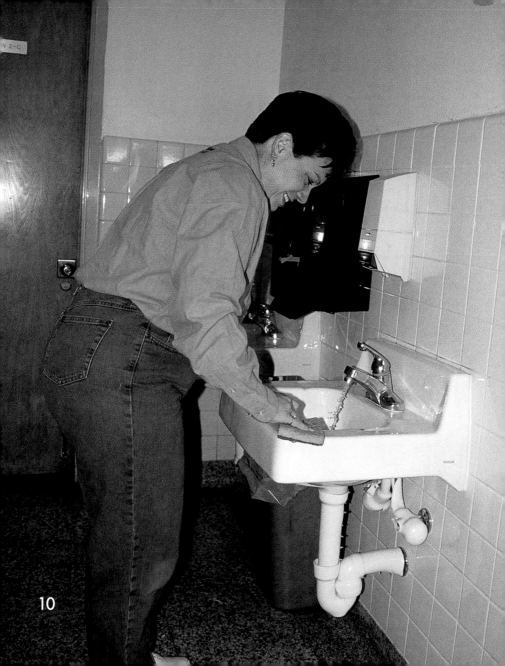

Custodians clean bathrooms.

Custodians dust shelves.

Custodians use
vacuum cleaners.

Custodians use mops.

Custodians use ladders.

Custodians keep schools clean and safe.

Words to Know

dust—to clean a coating of dirt from a surface; custodians dust desks, shelves, and other surfaces.

gather—to collect things; custodians gather trash from wastebaskets.

ladder—a metal or wooden tool that people climb to reach high places

sweep—to clean a floor with a broom; custodians sweep floors before they mop floors.

trash—things that people throw away

vacuum cleaner—a machine that picks up dirt from floors; custodians use vacuum cleaners to clean carpets.

Read More

Alphin, Elaine Marie. *Vacuum Cleaners.* Household History. Minneapolis: Carolrhoda Books, 1997.

Flanagan, Alice K. *Call Mr. Vasquez, He'll Fix It!* Our Neighborhood. New York: Children's Press, 1996.

Parker, Steve. *What's Inside Buildings?* What's Inside? New York: P. Bedrick Books, 1995.

Internet Sites

Janitors and Cleaners and Cleaning Supervisors
http://stats.bls.gov/oco/ocos174.htm

Training Your Custodians
http://www.spmmag.com/articles/Training.html

Index/Word List

Word Count: 33
Early-Intervention Level: 8

Editorial Credits
Martha E. H. Rustad, editor; Abby Bradford, Bradfordesign, Inc., cover designer; Kia Bielke, production designer; Kimberly Danger, photo researcher

Photo Credits
Kim Stanton, 6, 8, 10
M & M Photography/Matt Swinden, cover, 14, 18
Marilyn Moseley LaMantia, 12, 16
Mike Malyszko/FPG International LLC, 1
Monica Mark, 20
Shaffer Photography/James L. Shaffer, 4